♥ Mrs. Grossman's
BASIC STICKER IDEA BOOK™

Complete How-to Book for Designing Cards, Gift Wrap and Crafts with Stickers!

Mrs. Grossman wishes to thank the following artists
who have contributed original designs to this book:
Linda Risbrudt, Linda Hendrickson,
Audrey Giorgi, Julie Cohen, Melissa Carlson,
Susan Pratt, Gigi Sproul, Sue Ferguson,
Susanna Gallisdorfer and Judy Black.

Written by Mary Liz Curtin and Mary Clasen.
Instructions by Linda Hendrickson
Designed by Susan Pratt, Melissa Carlson,
Julie Cohen, Gigi Sproul and Andrea Grossman
with help from Blythe Omick and Raul Chacon.
Photography by Waldo Bascom.
Styling by Angie Heinrich.

Many thanks to the following people who have
offered ideas, counsel and encouragement:
Calvin Goodman, Patti Johnson, Bonnie Loizos,
Dee and Warren Gruenig.

Printed in the United States of America

Library of Congress Catalog Number: 97-93546
Mrs. Grossman's Paper Company
Mrs. Grossman's Basic Sticker Idea Book
ISBN: 0-910299013

Published by Mrs. Grossman's Paper Company
3810 Cypress Drive, Petaluma, California 94954
Distributed in Canada by Pierre Belvédère
Distributed in Japan by Sony Plaza Co., Ltd.

TABLE OF CONTENTS

ALL ABOUT STICKERS

Here are some general terms, definitions and hints to make sticker art even more creative and fun. We also address some common questions: What is a sticker module? How do I find the stickers I want? Where should—and shouldn't—I put stickers? The answers are right here!

Regular **R**

Double Regular **DR**

Giant **G**

Extravagant **E**
Modules

Back printing

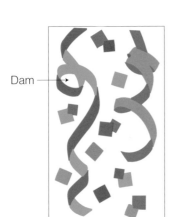
Dam —
Dams

Mirror Image

MODULE
Our entire line is based on a modular system. Module is the term for the sticker or stickers, between perforation marks. Some modules contain one sticker, while others contain an entire collection!

SIZE
Stickers come in sizes from micro flowers to extravagant rabbits. Some stickers, like the bear, are available in three sizes, but most are designed in the scale we found works best with other stickers.

LINER PAPER
This is the waxy paper stickers are on when you buy them. Save those liner papers! Later, you'll learn how to use them to build perfect sticker compositions.

BACK PRINTING
This is the information on back of the liner paper. Turn any Mrs. Grossman's sticker over and discover some great sticker ideas! You'll also find the name of the designer, a size and price code and the year the sticker was created and copyrighted.

DAMS
These are small, extra pieces found inside sticker designs. Remove the dams before you put the sticker down. If you miss one, you get to say "dam!" and remove it with an X-ACTO knife.

MIRROR IMAGE
This refers to identical sticker shapes printed facing opposite directions. This allows you to maximize flexibility in your sticker art, and place stickers back-to-back for 3-D designs.

MATERIAL
This is the type of paper used to make a sticker. Most of our stickers are printed on shiny, high-gloss paper. Some are printed with special film, materials and techniques.

4

Stickers are like smiles: They get your idea across without words.

HOW DO I AVOID TEARING STICKERS?
When removing stickers, start at the bottom and lift upwards, slowly peeling the sticker off the liner paper. If a sticker is difficult to remove, try bending the liner paper back first. With long or skinny stickers, lift part of the image, bend the liner paper back, press the exposed section in place, then peel up the rest of the liner paper.

WHERE CAN I PUT STICKERS?
Stickers really love paper! Cards, envelopes, gift bags, gift wrap, lunch bags, stationery—you name it! They can be used on other surfaces, too. However, we do not recommend placing stickers on furniture, painted walls, silk, leather, suede or vinyl.

OOPS! HOW DO I REMOVE STICKERS?
On wood or glass, apply some light furniture or salad oil, let it sit for a few minutes, then peel off the sticker. For other surfaces, we recommend using one of the gentle commercial solvent products available.

WHAT IS A COPYRIGHT?
Every Mrs. Grossman's sticker has been created by a trained designer, and is protected legally by a copyright. This means our stickers are meant to be used and enjoyed for personal use—but cannot be reproduced or sold on any item for commercial purposes.

HOW DO I FIND THE STICKERS I WANT?
Our stickers are sold in stationery and specialty stores, card shops, toy and craft stores and mail-order catalogs. Need help finding the stickers you want in your area? Call us at 800-429-4549 or visit our Website at www.mrsgross-mans.com

ARE THESE STICKERS ACID FREE?
Mrs. Grossman's frequently submits all of our materials to an independent lab for pH testing. The results verify that our stickers are virtually acid free. Our stickers should be safe for use in photo albums as long as the stickers are not placed directly on the photos. The subject of creating "archival" photo albums is a complicated one, and there are many factors to be aware of. We invite you to send for our complimentary info sheet, "Facts, Fiction and Fun: Helpful Tips on Scrapbooking".

TOOLS

Having the right tools at hand allows you to create effective, professional-looking sticker art with ease. We recommend the following tools:

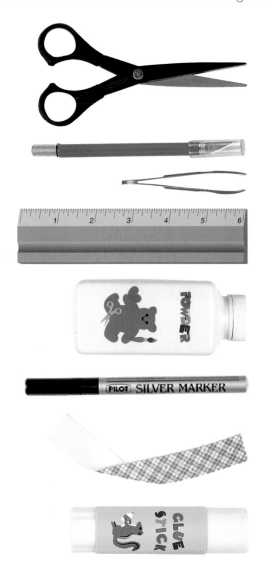

SCISSORS   A pair of good quality scissors is your most important tool, the one absolute essential. They should be sharp, maneuverable, comfortable and pointy, with long blades.

X-ACTO KNIFE   Craft knives are great for lifting and placing stickers (especially tiny pieces) as well as trimming stickers and paper. You can also use this knife with a ruler to cut stickers perfectly straight. Caution! These blades are really sharp so be extra careful and always put the cover on when not in use.

TWEEZERS   Pointy tweezers will help you move small pieces and reach into tight areas. They are useful for lifting stickers and placing them just where you want them.

RULER   A straight edge is often helpful to measure, center a design or help establish your ground line.

POWDER   What do you do when you don't want a sticker to stick? Put powder or cornstarch on the back to neutralize the adhesive.

PAINT PEN   Indispensable for adding sparkle and charm to your sticker art, these pens will write on even the shiniest surfaces. We recommend silver, gold and black.

MOUNTING TAPE   Give your stickers a lift! Mounting tape makes them rise off the page and gives your sticker art dimension.

GLUE STICK or DOUBLE STICK TAPE   Not everything we use is sticky! Keep this on hand to attach different colored papers or accessories to your sticker art.

MRS. GROSSMAN'S STICKER COMPANIONS   Choose from a rainbow of colorful bags, bookmarks and cards designed expressly for use with our stickers. Keep a supply of colored cards, paper and envelopes on hand.

FUN EXTRAS   Thread, ribbon, string, paper punches, deckle scissors and specialty papers are great accessories for your sticker art.

STICKER STORAGE

Simplify project set-up by storing stickers in a box by category. Keep stickers clean, dry and away from light, and they'll last indefinitely! To get you started, we recommend a sturdy box, separated into the following categories:

Hearts	Party	Accessories
Animals	Holiday	Flowers
Nature	Sports	Words and symbols

Keep an ample supply of the stickers you use frequently, and always file away a few favorites and extras of any new styles.

Any large box with a lid can hold a sticker collection, but none beats our Sticker File Box™. The dividers allow you to file by category so you can find the stickers you want when you want them. The lid keeps them dry, dust free and stays open while you work. Your tools will fit in the box, too.

A small collection (or portable collection for travel) will fit in an envelope or a document folder.

A three-ring binder is another good storage method. Use archival pocket pages in the binder to avoid damaging the stickers.

CUTTING

Cutting is a basic sticker art technique. You can use scissors or an X-ACTO knife. Some of us prefer one tool for everything, while others vary the tool as needed.

The rabbit used in this project extends past the boundaries of the card. Put it on the card, still on the liner paper, so you can decide where to place it. You will be able to see the border of the card through the sticker. Mark the cutting line with a ruler and pencil.

CUTTING WITH SCISSORS

Keep the line clean and straight as you cut this large sticker. Always leave your stickers on the liner paper when you cut them to keep your scissors clean.

CUTTING WITH A KNIFE

An X-ACTO knife makes a very clean cut, and is especially handy for avoiding choppy edges on larger stickers. Put the sticker on the card and place the ruler along the border. Draw the edge of the knife along the ruler and remove leftover pieces.

LIFTING

Pull stickers off the liner paper slowly to avoid tearing them. Watch out for those rabbit ears!

POWDERING

When you don't want a sticker—or part of a sticker—to stick, use powder or cornstarch to neutralize the adhesive. Pat it gently on the back of the sticker and wipe off the excess from the sticker and card. We use it here behind the rabbit's ear to make it look floppy.

Cutting with scissors

Cutting with a knife

Lifting

Powdering

This section is filled with tricks-of-the-trade and practice projects. We've chosen some fun designs to illustrate the basic techniques.

■ ■

BACK-TO-BACK

These balloons not only rise above the picture, but look good on both sides. Almost all of Mrs. Grossman's stickers are printed in mirror image to make it easy to achieve this effect.

Place the first balloon so that it extends above the card. Open the card and put another balloon behind the first one, lining up the edges and sticking the bottom of the balloon to inside of the card. The second balloon can be a different color.

Back to back

EMBELLISHMENTS

The balloon string here is drawn freehand with a paint pen or permanent marker. If you prefer, use a ruler to make the strings appear taut.

For a more dimensional look, use real string or ribbon for the balloon strings. Use your knife to cut around his paw, lift the paw up and slip the ribbon or string underneath. Tuck the other end under the bottom of the balloons.

Using a pen

Using a paint pen

3-D EFFECTS

Stickers that pop off the page add even more dimension to your work. Use a small piece of mounting tape on the back of the sticker, leaving the protective backing on the tape. Powder the back of the sticker, but not the tape. Remove the backing from the tape and press the sticker to the card.

FINAL

Congratulations! You've made a delightful card, perfect for any party!

3-dimensional

Finished card

9

There's one more essential skill for sticker art: learning which sticker to put on the surface first.

Here are very simple designs, shown step-by-step to help you practice the order in which to apply your stickers. If you need to lift a sticker—or part of a sticker—that is already in place, use your X-ACTO knife or a corner of the liner paper. Then you'll be able to slip the next sticker underneath.

This section also helps you remember to group your stickers. Keep the action together! As you copy these designs, think about how you would change them to make them your own.

Near each design you will find the names of the stickers used and the techniques employed. Sometimes we only use one or two stickers from a module. Save those extra stickers. Refer to the sticker list in the back of the book to identify the modules.

BUILDING WITH STICKERS
Here's an easy trick to help you build perfect sticker combinations before they even touch down! Choose stickers that will convey your message, provide a focal point or main character and supply a fun setting. Ready? Now try these two techniques for adjusting the placement of each sticker as you build:

Fingertips
Build simple combinations on your fingertips, adjusting the stickers until the image is picture perfect, then place your design on the desired surface.

Liner Paper
Build more complex designs on a large piece of liner paper, (save those Extravagant module liner papers!) Rebuild to your heart's content, then place the design.

Fingertips   Liner paper

FLOWER POT
African Daisies, Gardeners.

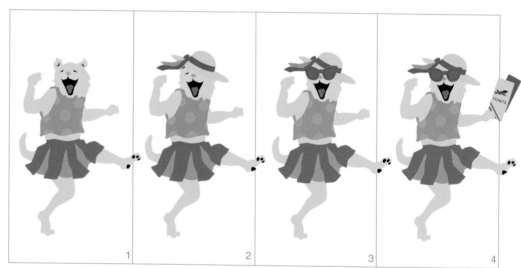

TRAVELING CAT
Expression Cat, Travel Gear.

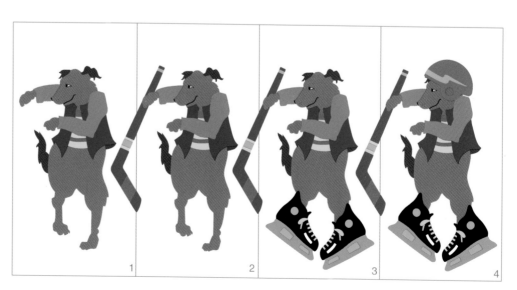

HOCKEY DOG
Expression Dog, Hockey.

BASKET OF FLOWERS
Basket, Bouquet, Multi Bows.
1. Cut the back handle of the basket as shown. 2. Place the bouquet behind the basket and reposition the handle. 3. Trim the excess. 4. Place the bow.

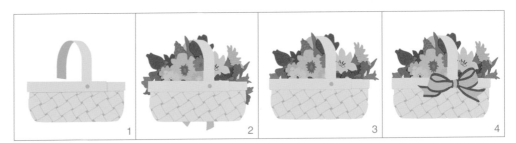

COMPUTER MONKEY
Computer, Monkeys.
1. Position the computer. 2. Place the sitting monkey at the computer. 3. Cut the hanging monkey so his head fits in the computer screen. 4. Add the mouse.

FLOWER BOUQUET
Tulip, Pink Phlox, Multi Bows.
1. Cut the tulip as shown. 2. Place the phlox with the stem behind the tulip. 3. Add the second tulip. 4. Add the bow.

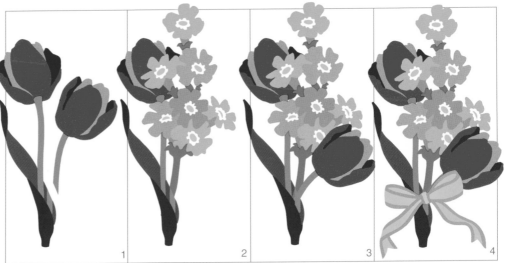

MECHANIC FROG
Frogs, Car, Tools.
1. Cut the frog and hammer as shown.
2. Place the frog under car, add the arm.
3. Add the hammer piece as a jack and place the screwdriver.

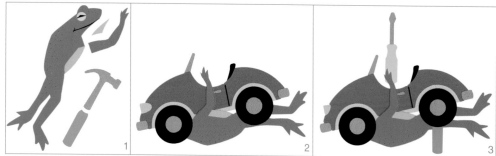

SKATING MANTIS
Insects, Snow Gear.
1. Cut the insect and scarf as shown.
2. Place the skate on the cut leg.
3. Arrange the body. 4. Add the other skate, scarf and hat.

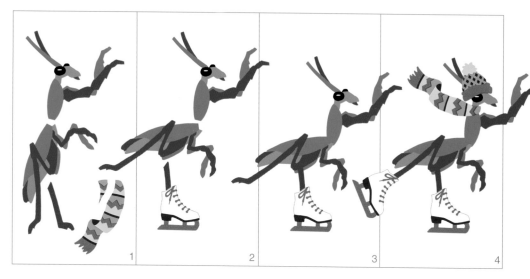

GARDENING RABBIT
Giant Green Thumb, Daffodils.
1. Cut the rabbit as shown. 2. Arrange the rabbit. 3. Place the daffodils.

DESIGN BASICS

PLACEMENT
You will find it is easy to create effective designs when you learn how to combine and position stickers on a card.

By grouping your sticker images you create visual order in your picture. Then the space around and between stickers (negative space) brings attention to the stickered image (focal point).

You can position your sticker images on the card in the center...

on a diagonal...

to the edge of the card...

or beyond the edge.

PLANNING
Have a plan before you start stickering. Know what you want to say and select the stickers that suit your message

As you plan your composition, hold the stickers over the card to see exactly where you want to place them. Put them down lightly in case you want to move one or tuck one sticker behind another.

Do the unexpected! Add drama and motion to your design. In this design we have torn a red heart and placed a few small balloons to suggest movement.

Mrs. Grossman's stickers are purposely made to be used together, so designing is simple, and the possibilities are limitless! Start by practicing the four basic concepts shown here: placement, planning, depth and story. Then add the most important element—your personal touch—to make the images come to life!

DEPTH
Stickers scattered all over the card appear to float.

Placing stickers together in a group gives your design a sense of depth.

A ground line (horizontal line or plane) gives your sticker image a place to rest.

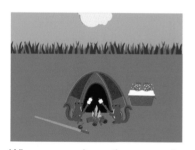

Where you place the ground line will convey distance...

or closeness.

It can be a drawn line or an imaginary one.

TELL A STORY
Use stickers to tell a story! Here's a boy heading off to school.

Here's a lucky couple going off on their honeymoon.

This Fourth of July parade uses all of the Design Basics to tell a happy story.

BEYOND THE BASICS

What's the secret to creating advanced sticker art? Just combine the techniques, design skills and special effects you've learned—all in one project! Here are some examples:

POP-UP, OUT AND OFF
- 3-D effects with mounting tape
- Trimmed, nested, decorated bags
- Powdered, over the edge stickers
- Dimensional sticker shadows
- Real string

STAND UP AND STAND OUT
- Simple, eye-catching design
- Back-to-back stickers
- Prominent placement
- Whimsical character

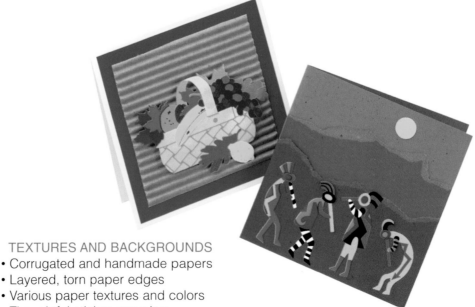

TEXTURES AND BACKGROUNDS
- Corrugated and handmade papers
- Layered, torn paper edges
- Various paper textures and colors
- Thoughtful sticker grouping

READY SET STICKER!

In the rest of this book, you'll follow colorful examples, read step-by-step instructions—and create amazing sticker art!

The sections ahead offer six exciting themes: Birthday, School and Sports, At Home, Flowers, Baby and Photo Albums. Each section includes sticker art activities and photos, useful tips, and an entire page of extra design ideas. Some projects have detailed instructions, while others are so straightforward, you can simply copy the picture.

YOU'RE THE ARTIST

Remember, the ideas in this book are just the beginning! There's no end to the creative projects you can make with stickers. It's okay to change and rearrange stickers to make your own brand new designs. So go ahead. Explore uncharted territories! Throw away the map!

DETAILS, DETAILS, DETAILS
- Multiple ground lines
- Trimmed, nested gift bags
- Thoughtful placement and grouping
- 3-D effects with mounting tape
- Powdered, over the edge stickers
- Dimensional sticker shadows
- Layered stickers

FUN WITH FOUR OR FEWER

Sticker art is for everybody! It's fun, quick and clean. Best of all, whether you use five or fifty stickers, your designs will always be a delight to make, give, and receive. Start with these projects that get the message across with less than five stickers.

FRIENDLY ADVICE

- Set up the work area so stickers and tools are handy.
- Flip back to the front sections if you need a refresher course.
- It's okay to experiment and change designs.
- It's okay to cut or use part of a sticker.
- It's okay to overlap stickers.
- It's okay to enjoy yourself!

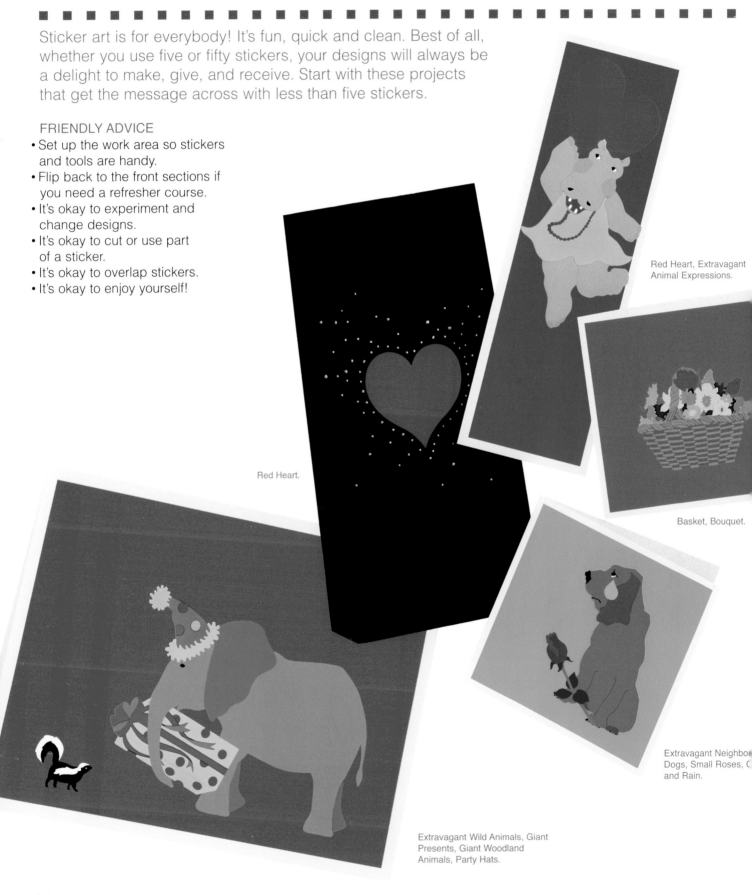

Red Heart, Extravagant Animal Expressions.

Red Heart.

Basket, Bouquet.

Extravagant Neighbor Dogs, Small Roses, and Rain.

Extravagant Wild Animals, Giant Presents, Giant Woodland Animals, Party Hats.

It doesn't take much to make magic with stickers.

Giant Bear, Balloon, Cloud and Rain.

Tulip, Ivy.

Penguin, Sparkle Small Heart.

Extravagant Animal Expressions.

Extravagant Neighborhood Dogs, Giant Cats, Sparkle Hugs and Kisses, Sparkle Multi Micro Hearts.

Sorry — I forgot!

BIRTHDAY

GIFT CARD
Giant Presents, Multi Bows, Micro Flowers, Bear. Cluster the flowers together, add the bow and place it in the bears paw.

BIRTHDAY CARD
Confetti, Balloons, Giant Presents, Opalescent Sun, Moon and Stars.
Cut the balloons at different angles and place them on the card. Place the presents to achieve depth. Finish it off with a silver paint pen.

MINI PARTY BAG
Small Balloons, Party Hats, Giant Presents, Extravagant Animal Expressions, Parties and Toys.
Place the present in the position shown. Add Pippa using mounting tape. Attach the silver threads to the balloons and tuck them behind Pippa's hand. Use mounting tape to attach the balloons and powder the backs where they extend over the edge.

PARTY HAT
Balloons, Confetti, Small Bear, Bear, Giant Bear, Party Hats, Small Presents, Pinwheel, Party.
For this wonderful hat, place a smaller bear in the giant bear's arm and tuck another one behind him. Cut the confetti into shorter lengths. Add the confetti, hats, presents and pinwheel. Powder the giant bear's left paw and the tops of both of the bears. Attach the balloons back-to-back on colored wire and insert into the top of the hat.

Stickers add sparkle and cheer to every celebration—especially Birthday parties! From colorful cards and gift wrap to party hats, place settings and favor bags; stickers personalize and brighten that special day. Create a coordinated theme by repeating the same design on all of your party accessories.

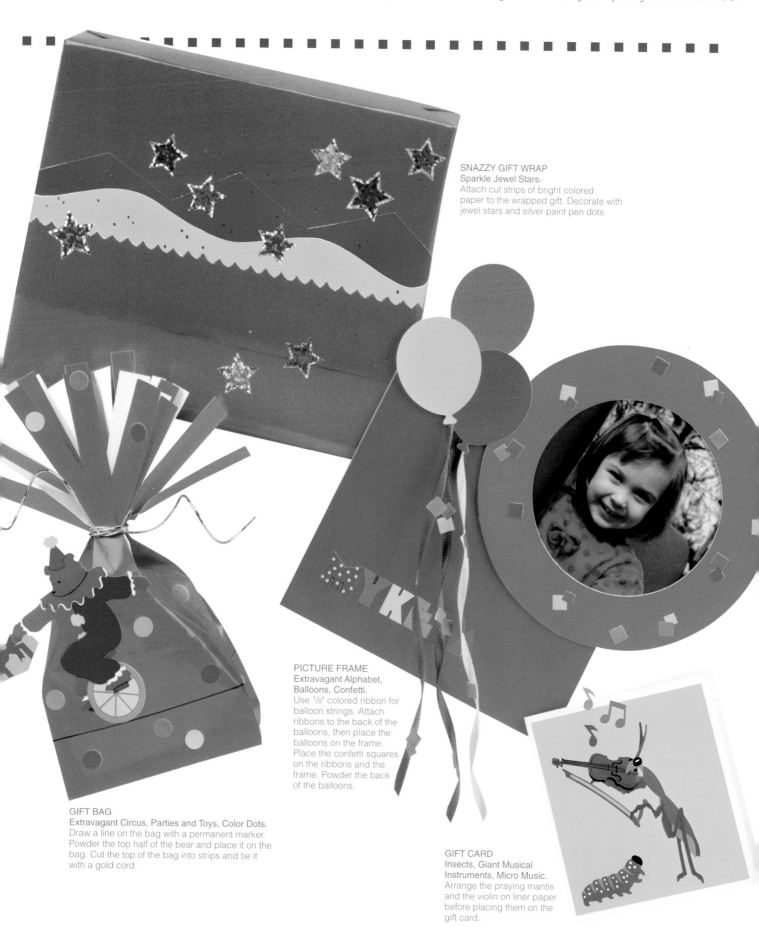

SNAZZY GIFT WRAP
Sparkle Jewel Stars.
Attach cut strips of bright colored paper to the wrapped gift. Decorate with jewel stars and silver paint pen dots.

PICTURE FRAME
Extravagant Alphabet, Balloons, Confetti.
Use 1/8" colored ribbon for balloon strings. Attach ribbons to the back of the balloons, then place the balloons on the frame. Place the confetti squares on the ribbons and the frame. Powder the back of the balloons.

GIFT BAG
Extravagant Circus, Parties and Toys, Color Dots.
Draw a line on the bag with a permanent marker. Powder the top half of the bear and place it on the bag. Cut the top of the bag into strips and tie it with a gold cord.

GIFT CARD
Insects, Giant Musical Instruments, Micro Music.
Arrange the praying mantis and the violin on liner paper before placing them on the gift card.

BIRTHDAY CARD
Extravagant Alphabet, Micro Music Notes, Opalescent Sun, Moon and Stars.

Start with the H and A in Happy, then continue placing letters on a curving ground line. Add the music notes, and finish with silver paint pen dots. Don't forget the envelope!

PLACE SETTING
Extravagant Wild Animals, Extravagant Alphabet, Party, Small Wild Animals, Color Dots, Micro Stars, Balloons, Charms.

Cut and nest three mini bags to create the giraffe's home. Powder the back of the giraffe's head and neck for dimension. Coordinate the plate, napkin ring and cup with the other wild animals.

BIRTHDAY CAKE
Extravagant Carousel Animals, Color Dots.

Place carousel animals back-to-back on plastic skewers. Decorate the cake with the skewers and long, thin candles. Keep the candles away from the stickers. Use color dots to add zip to the cake plate.

PARTY FAVOR BAGS
Extravagant Neighborhood Dogs, Extravagant Carousel Animals, Giant Bear, Giant Beach, Party Hats, Color Dots, Balloon, Clown, Multi Bows, Grass, Parties and Toys.

Cut the mini bags as shown. Add stickers and nest the bags. Powder the stickers where they extend over the edge. Attach the clown, horse, balloons and party hat with mounting tape. Use two bows to make the bear's bow tie pop up. Draw the balloon string with a permanent marker.

Any sticker idea can be used on a variety of surfaces. These easy combinations are waiting for you to decide where to use them.

SCHOOL AND SPORTS

MEMO PAD
Classroom Stuff, Small Alphabet, Gymnastics, Super Stars, Dessert.

BOOKMARKS
Extravagant Neighborhood Dogs, Books, Small Apples, Small Alphabet, Giant Cats, Classroom Stuff, School, Travel Gear, Expression Dog.
Arrange the stickers on a piece of liner paper, then place them.

GIFT CARD
Graduation Hats, Panda, Micro Flowers, Blurb.
Hand write a message on the blurb. Cut the panda's arm to hold the diploma.

REPORT FOLDER
Sparkle Rocket Ships, Sparkle Space, Opalescent Colored Circles, Extravagant Celestial, Frogs, Opalescent Sun, Moon and Stars, Extravagant Alphabet.

RULER
Small Alphabet, Micro Stars.

For years, teachers, parents, coaches and doctors have been giving children stickers as rewards for special achievements. This section features many other fantastic projects that are guaranteed to "make the grade" with kids of all ages!

ALL STAR ANIMALS
Baseball Gear, Extravagant Neighborhood Dogs, Giant Beach.
Cut the white dog's mouth and the tan dog's paw so they can hold their equipment.

GIFT CARD
Hockey, Panda, Opalescent Sun, Moon and Stars.

GOLF CARD
Expressions Dog, Cat and Bear, Golf, Giant Trees, Opal Sun, Moon and Stars, Baseball.
Cut a green card or paper and glue it to a blue card to make the golf course.

KEY CHAIN
Sports, Micro Stars.

FRAME
Penguin, Baseball, Confetti Stars, Micro Stars, Extravagant Alphabet.

25

CALENDAR

Extravagant Neighborhood Dogs, Calendar Stickers, Confetti Stars, Soccer, Hockey, Golf, Football, Gymnastics, Basketball, Baseball, Sports, Elephant, Expression Bear, Insects, Super Stars.

Print a blank calendar on your computer and use stickers to mark appointments, activities and special days. Later, these pages are a marvelous addition to your memory book.

BOOK COVERS

Extravagant Neighborhood Dogs, Extravagant Geometrics, Blurbs, Small Alphabet, Small Numbers, Super Stars, Insects, Frogs, Monkeys, Basketball Gear. Use bright, heavy paper to cover the books. Decorate them with your favorite sticker characters and make a bookmark to match.

LUNCH BOX

Extravagant Neighborhood Dogs, Giant Picnic, Fast Food, Basket, Fruit, Micro Butterflies, Cloud and Rain, Extravagant Animal Expressions.

Assemble the stickers on liner paper, and apply them to the lunch box.

CERTIFICATE

Extravagant Geometrics, Gymnastics, Best Ribbon, Micro Stars.

Use your computer to make a certificate and print it on colorful paper. Apply the stickers to make it a very special award.

Stickers make the grade with all ages! Use them to design colorful flash cards.

Class of '97

DISHWASHER MAGNETS
Opalescent Fish, Confetti, Small Alphabet, Opalescent Party Glasses, Hockey, Tea Set, Giant Picnic, Giant Camping, Cooks, Frame Kit.

Magnets are attached to the back of these designs. Cut the confetti to fit.

GIFT CARD
Bear, Basket, Sewing.
Cut the back handle of the basket before you fill it. Arrange the design on liner paper, wrap a piece of thread around it then place it on the card.

NOTEBOOK
Extravagant Rabbit, Extravagant Alphabet, Books, Pens and Crayon.
Cut the rabbit's paws to hold the books. Arrange the design on liner paper and place it on book.

CHANGE OF ADDRESS CARD
Small Alphabet, Giant House, Giant Trees, Extravagant Animal Expressions, Telephone, Travel Gear, Wagon, Extravagant Furniture, Sports, Giant Pet Shop, Bicycle.
Cut around Pippa's cheek to position the phone. Mounting tape behind Pippa and the full wagon adds depth.

Chances are, if you have a home craft project, you can make it more exciting by adding stickers! Use them to decorate, organize and label household items. From recipe cards and stationery, to luggage tags and refrigerator magnets, stickers make everyday life a little more fun!

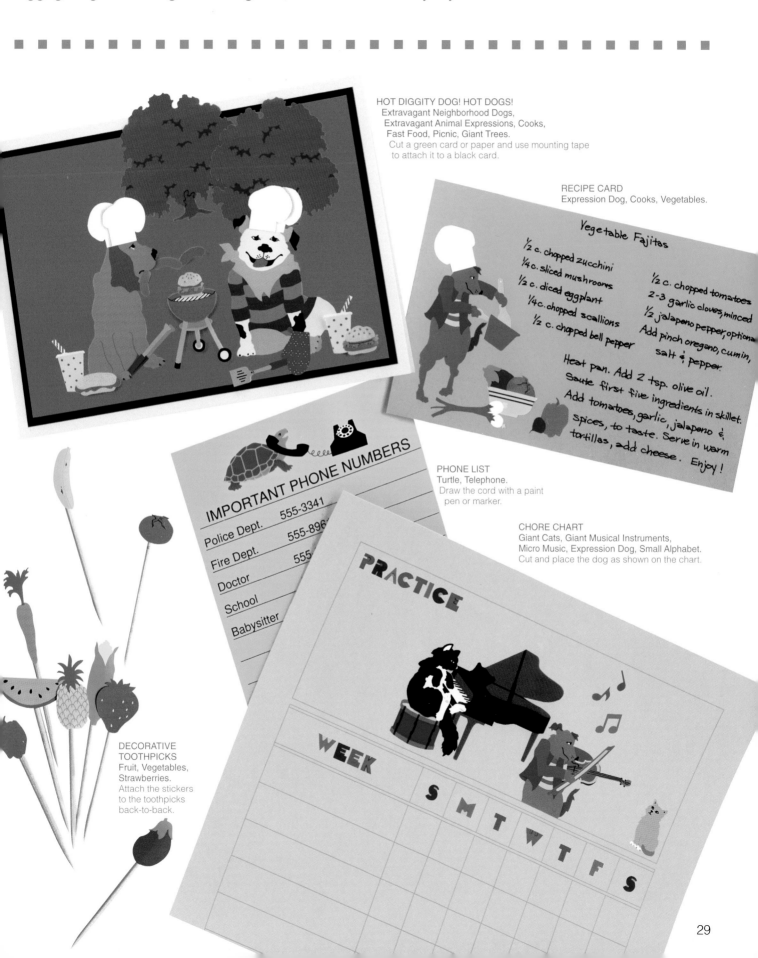

HOT DIGGITY DOG! HOT DOGS!
Extravagant Neighborhood Dogs, Extravagant Animal Expressions, Cooks, Fast Food, Picnic, Giant Trees.
Cut a green card or paper and use mounting tape to attach it to a black card.

RECIPE CARD
Expression Dog, Cooks, Vegetables.

Vegetable Fajitas

½ c. chopped zucchini
¼ c. sliced mushrooms
½ c. diced eggplant
¼ c. chopped scallions
½ c. chopped bell pepper

½ c. chopped tomatoes
2-3 garlic cloves, minced
½ jalapeno pepper, optional
Add pinch oregano, cumin, salt & pepper.

Heat pan. Add 2 tsp. olive oil. Saute first five ingredients in skillet. Add tomatoes, garlic, jalapeno & spices, to taste. Serve in warm tortillas, add cheese. Enjoy!

IMPORTANT PHONE NUMBERS

Police Dept.	555-3341
	555-896
Fire Dept.	555-
Doctor	
School	
Babysitter	

PHONE LIST
Turtle, Telephone.
Draw the cord with a paint pen or marker.

CHORE CHART
Giant Cats, Giant Musical Instruments, Micro Music, Expression Dog, Small Alphabet.
Cut and place the dog as shown on the chart.

PRACTICE

WEEK   S M T W T F S

DECORATIVE TOOTHPICKS
Fruit, Vegetables, Strawberries.
Attach the stickers to the toothpicks back-to-back.

TIP: *Laminate your stickered luggage tags, recipe cards and other frequently used items for durability.*

HOMEMADE TAGS

Quilting Gear, Quilt Patterns, Bear, Buttons, Sewing, Basket.

Cut sturdy colored paper with craft scissors into rectangles, some a bit larger than others. Glue smaller rectangles to contrasting larger ones. Punch a hole in the corner and add ribbons.

HOME OFFICE

Quilting Gear, Sewing, Elves, Travel, Small Alphabet, Turtle, Small Numbers, Make-up.

Use stickers to add color and charm to business cards, notes, stationery—even your to-do list.

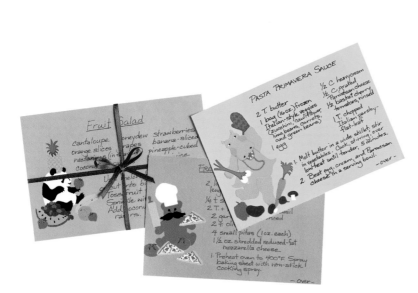

RECIPE CARDS

Panda, Fruit, Bear, Cooks, Fast Food, Vegetables, Extravagant Animal Expressions.

Write your favorite family recipes on stickered cards to create a gift straight from the heart.

SELF-MAILER INVITATION

Reflection Tree, Sparkle Micro Stars.

Take one light and one dark piece of paper. Hold them together and cut the top edges with craft scissors. (Save trim from dark paper.) On your computer print the invitation. Glue the papers together with the light paper extending 1/8" above the dark paper. Glue the leftover trimmed strip to the bottom of the light paper as shown. Add stickers to the inside. Fold as shown and seal with reflection tree. Add sparkle stars.

Finally! Something sticky a homemaker can enjoy!

FLOWERS

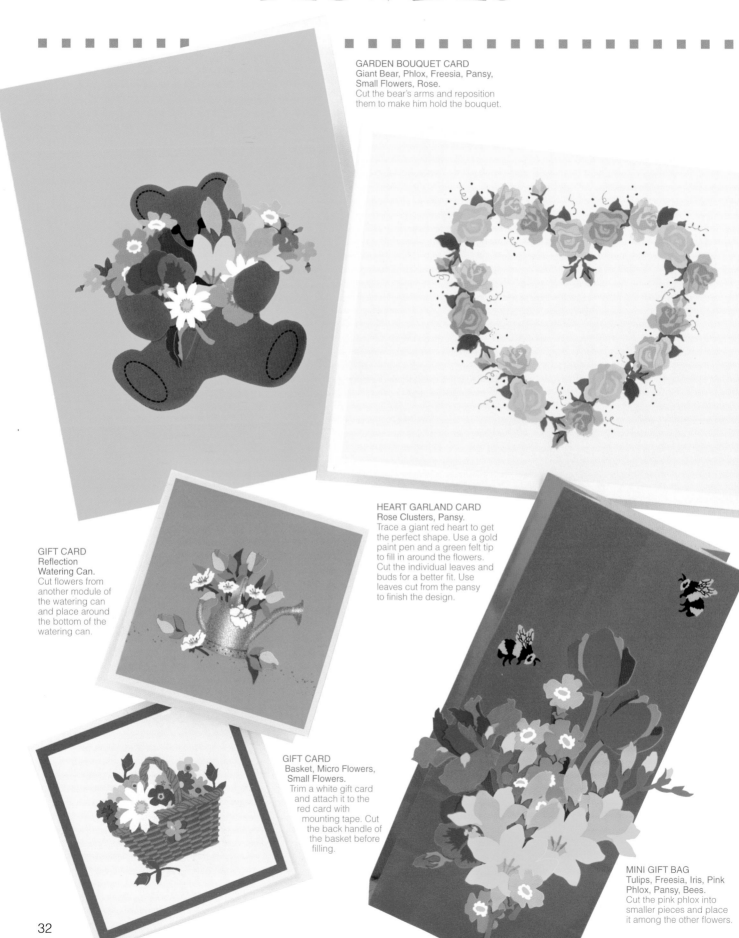

GARDEN BOUQUET CARD
Giant Bear, Phlox, Freesia, Pansy,
Small Flowers, Rose.
Cut the bear's arms and reposition
them to make him hold the bouquet.

GIFT CARD
Reflection
Watering Can.
Cut flowers from
another module of
the watering can
and place around
the bottom of the
watering can.

HEART GARLAND CARD
Rose Clusters, Pansy.
Trace a giant red heart to get
the perfect shape. Use a gold
paint pen and a green felt tip
to fill in around the flowers.
Cut the individual leaves and
buds for a better fit. Use
leaves cut from the pansy
to finish the design.

GIFT CARD
Basket, Micro Flowers,
Small Flowers.
Trim a white gift card
and attach it to the
red card with
mounting tape. Cut
the back handle of
the basket before
filling.

MINI GIFT BAG
Tulips, Freesia, Iris, Pink
Phlox, Pansy, Bees.
Cut the pink phlox into
smaller pieces and place
it among the other flowers.

What could be more beautiful than a bouquet of flowers that blooms forever? Fanciful flowers are a favorite at Mrs. Grossman's—and you can see why! No matter what the season, Spring will last all year with these lovely designs.

BOOKMARK
Sunflower, Micro Butterflies.
Place the sunflowers on the bookmark and then cut lightly along the border with a craft knife.

GREETING CARD
Giant Garden, Bouquet.

GIFT BOX
Daffodils, Grass, Micro Flowers, Micro Butterflies.
Place daffodils and micro flowers on the wrapped gift and then add the grass.

STATIONERY
Confetti, Micro Flowers.

Linda Summers
29 Dutch Valley Rd.
San Francisco, CA 95120

Danielle Johnson
4620 Evergreen Court
San Mateo, CA 94516

USA Rose

33

FLOWER LABELS
Pansy, Micro Butterflies, Rose Garland,
Micro Flowers, Ivy.
Use the stickers of your choice to create sensational
labels.

WRAPPED GIFT
Bees, Tulips, Calla Lily, Pansy, Freesia, Iris, Sunflower,
Pink Phlox.
Wrap the gift and use any combination of flowers to
build a garden. Overlap and cut the flowers into

FLOWER TOTE AND GIFT CARD
Pink Phlox, Iris, Freesia, Tulip, Rose.
Start constructing the graceful arch from the left, one
flower at a time. Cut the stems off to get the correct
proportions. Cut the iris in half and use it in both places.

BLOOMING STATIONERY
Sunflower, African Daisy, Ivy, Small Flowers, Tulip,
Micro Flowers, Multi Bows.
Place matching sticker designs on note cards and
envelopes. A decorated box filled with floral stationery
is a marvelous gift.

Use flower stickers on note paper, cards and gifts all year-round.

BABY

PICTURE FRAME
Opalescent Sun, Moon and Stars,
Clouds and Rain, Extravagant Baby.

TODDLER CUP
Extravagant Baby.
This cup has a removable insert
for decorating. Make the design
on yellow paper and place
it inside the clear outer
sleeve.

GIFT CARD
Extravagant Baby, Basket.
Cut the back handle of the basket
for easy placement of the stickers.
Fill the basket before placing it on the
gift card.

CONGRATULATIONS
Extravagant Baby.
Cut a white card and use mounting tape to attach it to
a pink card. Mounting tape is also used on the bear, and
a double layer on the blocks to add depth. Cut the bear's arm
to the top of the diaper so it can hold the rabbit.

GIFT TAG
Small Ducks, Micro Hearts.
Cut a piece of colored paper with scissors to create
the water. Place the stickers on the background card
and use mounting tape on the water to attach it.

These projects are quick, easy and absolutely enchanting! Personalize nursery necessities with a repeated design, or help older siblings put stickers on birth announcements. Have a little more time? Decorate your baby album, create captivating thank you notes—or make a unique shower gift for a friend.

GIFT BAG
Extravagant Baby, Opalescent Sun, Moon and Stars, Cloud and Rain.
Punch a hole into the top of a folded bag for the ribbon. Arrange the bear and clouds on liner paper, then place on the bag.

GIFT CARD
Extravagant Baby, Bear.
Cut the bow off of the bib and place on the bear's head.

GIFT CARD
Extravagant Baby. Small Bears.

GIFT WRAP
Baby Clothesline.
Cut the blanket to create the borders. Draw the hangers with a permanent pen.

BABY BOOK
Extravagant Baby, Opalescent Sun, Moon and Stars.
Use stickers to enhance your baby book. Pink and blue are very nice, but babies like brights colors, too!

SHOWER INVITATION
Extravagant Baby.
Draw the clothesline with a paint pen or marker, then hang the toys, bottle and booties.

THREE DIMENSIONAL BEAR BOX
Extravagant Baby.
Place the bear snugly amid the bows for a fabulous package topper. Use the border along the bottom of the box, and finish it off with the other baby stickers. Attach the hearts to the ribbon ends.

PEEK-A-BOO BIRTH ANNOUNCEMENT
Opalescent Flower Garland.
Cut a circle out of the card and tape the picture on the inside looking out. Border the hole with the flower garland. Print the announcement on paper, cut it to fit and attach with mounting tape.

What is almost as cute as a baby's smile? Stickers in the nursery!

PHOTO ALBUMS

Plan your pages before you begin by placing the various elements on the page. Consider color copy enlargements instead of the original photographs. When everything is perfect, mount the images in the album.

Extravagant Geometrics, Bear, Pens, Pencils and Crayons, Balloons, Small Alphabet.

First Painting

one year old

1ST

Micro Stars, Extravagant Alphabet.

PARIS 1997

Extravagant Geometrics, Micro Stars, Gymnastics.

Photo albums will never be the same! Stickers enhance the family album by adding color and excitement, without "stealing the show." Mrs. Grossman's has stickers to enhance virtually every photograph. Before jumping into this project, be sure you have an extra copy of each print stored safely with the negatives—then let yourself go!

Extravagant Neighborhood Dogs, Giant Cats, Insects, Snow Gear, Travel Gear.

Extravagant Celestial, Sparkle Trout, Giant Woodland Animals, Grass, Small Train.

Baseball.

Extravagant Alphabet, Arrows, Extravagant Neighborhood Dogs.

41

TIP: *Be sure to make two copies of all your prints: store one with your negatives and use one in your album. Also, take more than one shot of an occasion so you can tell a story.*

Sparkle Trout, Giant Woodland Animals, Extravagant Celestial, Small Train.

Photo 1: Cut the photo as shown to create a dimensional effect. Extend the fishing pole line with a black marker. Add clouds (from small train), sparkle trout and sun.

Photo 2: Cut the person out of the photo and place in a new background. Add the woodland animals and grass.

Fast Food, Cooks, Desserts, Vegetables, Fruit, Giant Picnic.
Trim the chef's hat to fit the chef. Use a color copy of photo for this project.

Snow Tree, Snowman, Skiing.
Mount photo on colored paper. Cut the snow tree in half and position on either side of the photo. Arrange the skis and equipment. Add the snowballs.

Design Lines Checkerboard Plus, Basic Black and White, Extravagant Geometrics.
Cut the design lines to fit around the photo. Finish the corners with circles and squares.

Extravagant Geometrics.
Mount the photo on photo safe colored paper as shown. Add the stickers.

Rose with Ribbon, Reflection Small Hearts.
Tear a piece of paper a little larger than the photo. Mount on a contrasting piece of larger paper. Use a color copy of photo for this project. Add the stickers.

Palm Trees, Monkeys.
Place trees behind the photo. Add the monkeys and raffia to create an interesting frame. Use a color copy of photo for this project.

RESOURCES

Congratulations—you're an official sticker artist! You've learned basic techniques and design skills, made dozens of creative crafts and (hopefully) had a great time in the process. Want to know more? We recommend these resources for additional sticker art information and inspiration:

Holiday Sticker Idea Book

Sticker Express Newsletter

STICKER LINER PAPER
Start by checking the back of Mrs. Grossman's liner paper for fresh sticker design ideas.

HOLIDAY STICKER IDEA BOOK
A year-round guide for stickering fun! Filled with hundreds of new ideas; the ideal companion for the Basic Sticker Idea Book.

MRS. GROSSMAN'S VIDEOS
Watch the pros and learn their secrets! These dynamic, interactive videos demonstrate sticker art through friendly, hands-on projects.
• Sticker Magic
• Sticker Magic 2: *Creative Card Making*

STICKER EXPRESS NEWSLETTER
Let us deliver the latest sticker news to your home! Interested in a 6-issue yearly subscription? Call **800-429-4549** for more information.

MRS. GROSSMAN'S HOTLINE
Have questions? Can't find the right stickers? Stuck on a sticker project? Call **800-429-4549** for on-the-spot answers and advice.

VISIT OUR WEBSITE
A great resource for innovative stickering ideas and the latest news. Our address is: www.mrsgrossmans.com

Throughout this book, we have used Mrs. Grossman's cards, gift cards, bookmarks, bags and kits. Along with these we have used complimentary products manufactured and distributed by the following companies:
• Lunch box, Ice Man by Metro Kane page 26.
• Notes and envelopes, Crane and Co., pages 34, 38.
• Baby Shirt, Mervyn's, page 37.
• Papers and envelopes, The Paper Company, pages 30, 33, 34.
• Fiskars Paper Edgers, pages 21, 30, 36.

How does anyone make such beautiful stickers? You only need to have the best artists who work together as one talent, who love to design happy, uplifting and sometimes downright silly images and won't stop until the work is done and done *right*. It's simple!

Take, for instance, **Gigi Sproul**, top row right. She has worked at MGPC for more than sixteen years and delights us with her marvelous humor. No assignment is too difficult; she relishes a challange and has in fact, mastered all of the many facets of the art department.

Or **Melissa Carlson**, top row center, a creative dynamo in a gentle and sweet package. With MGPC for fourteen years, Melissa is our flower expert. But that's not all she does: she is equally proficient with package design and innovative product concepts.

Or **Susan Pratt**, top row left. A relative newcomer (only five years), Susan brings a graceful addition to the mix. Her years as a designer of children's clothing shows in her light-at-heart designs, but like Melissa, she loves variety and leaps at the opportunity to design new product.

Now **Julie Cohen**, bottom row left, has been with MGPC for fifteen years and is lovingly called "the Eye"- nothing gets by her. Even with an incredible eye for detail, she manages to get terrific energy and affection in her sticker designs.

Andrea Grossman, bottom row center, designed most of the original stickers (starting with the red heart in 1979) and now occasionally gets to design a new one. Her primary job as art director is to love these people- and *that* is a piece of cake.

Susanna Gallisdorfer, coming in from left field (where she spends a lot of her time), has designed stickers for years, many on staff, now by phone, mail and fax. Her stickers add a special whimsy to the line.

Now that you are acquainted, remember to look for the designers' names on the back of our stickers!

While they aren't pictured above, special credit goes to our terrific staff of support people: **Blythe Omick** and **Raul Chacon** take the designers' drawings from original to printable. **Linda Hendrickson** and **Audrey Giorgi** design original sticker art as well as numerous other creative assignments to produce what you see in this book.

STICKER CHECKLIST

Red Heart R	Micro Red&Pink Heart R	Small Red Heart R	Micro Hearts R	Spectrum Heart R	Quilted Heart R	Small Roses R	Rose DR	Pansy R	Sunflower DR	Phlox DR	Calla Lily DR	Freesia DR
Tulip DR	Iris DR	Rose w/Ribbon DR	Small Flowers R	African Daisy R	Rose Clusters R	Micro Flowers R	Bouquet R	Daffodils R	Ivy DR	Garden Border DR	Grass DR	Small Leaves R
Cloud and Rain R	Micro Stars R	Confetti Stars R	Gardening Tools DR	Gardeners R	Insects DR	Ladybugs R	Fruit DR	Vegetables DR	Palm Tree DR	Small Apples R	Apple R	Basket R
Colts R	Kittens R	Small Bears R	Bear R	Chipmunks R	Small Ducks R	Lambs R	Bunnies R	Bees R	Puppies R	Birds DR	Micro Butterflies R	Elephant R
Giraffe DR	Panda R	Monkeys DR	Small Wild Animals DR	Penguin R	Turtles R	Frogs R	Expressions Bear DR	Expressions Cat DR	Expressions Dog DR	Clown DR	Dancing Bear DR	
Color Dots R	Arrows R	Buttons R	Quilt Patterns R	Quilting Gear R	Sewing Gear R	Charms R	Tools R	Cooks R	Fast Food R	Desserts R	Tea Set DR	
Doctors and Nurses R	Make-up R	Computer R	Telephone R	Pens, Pencils R	Super Stars DR	Book R	Best Ribbon R	Graduation Hats R	Classroom Stuff DR	School DR	Small Flags R	
Travel Gear DR	Soccer R	Baseball R	Hockey R	Sports R	Football R	Golf R	Skiing R	Basketball R	Gymnastics DR	Snow Toys DR	Money R	

46

All the stickers we used in this book are shown here. This handy checklist makes it easy to find the stickers you need.

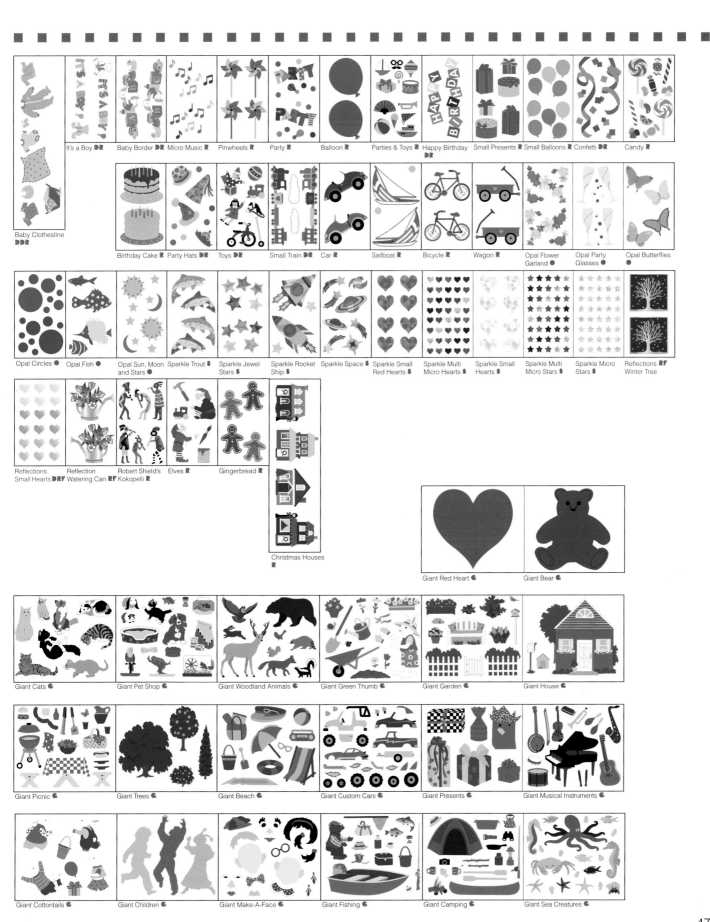

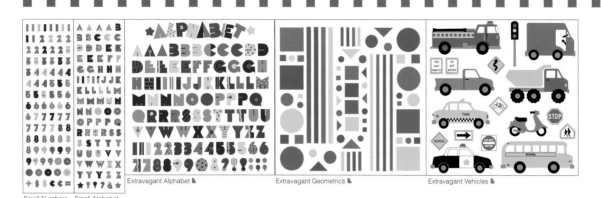

Small Numbers **DDR** Small Alphabet **DDR**

Extravagant Alphabet **E**

Extravagant Geometrics **E**

Extravagant Vehicles **E**

Extravagant Circus **E**

Extravagant Animal Expressions **E**

Extravagant Neighborhood Dogs **E**

Extravagant Wild Animals **E**

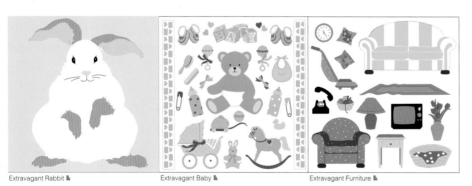

Extravagant Carousel Animals **E**

Extravagant Trim-a-Tree **E**

Extravagant Celestial **E**

Extravagant Rabbit **E**

Extravagant Baby **E**

Extravagant Furniture **E**

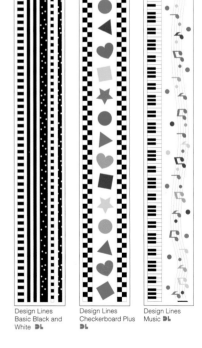

Design Lines Basic Black and White **DL**

Design Lines Checkerboard Plus **DL**

Design Lines Music **DL**

R	Regular	**S**	Sparkle
DR	Double Regular	**DS**	Double Sparkle
DDR	Double Double Regular	**DDS**	Double Double Sparkle
●	Opalescent	**RF**	Reflections

DRF	Double Reflections
G	Giant
E	Extravagant
DL	Design Lines